SPIRITUAL PARENTING

WHO'S ENTERING AND EXITING YOUR LIFE

DR. SHIRLEY R. BROWN, TH. D

FORWARD WRITE NOW PUBLISHING: A SUBSIDIARY OF
MAXIMUM SUCCESS LIVING, LLC

Copyright © 2019 by Dr. Shirley R. Brown, Th. D
All rights reserved.
Printed in the United States of America

ISBN: 978-0-9992640-2-7

Published by Forward Write Now Publishing, Wendell, North Carolina

No part of this book may be reproduced in any form or by any electronic or mechanical means, including information storage and retrieval systems, without written permission from the author, except for the use of brief quotations in a book review.

Scriptures marked KJV are taken from the KING JAMES VERSION (KJV): KING JAMES VERSION, public domain.

Scriptures marked NASB are taken from the NEW AMERICAN STANDARD (NAS): Scripture taken from the NEW AMERICAN STANDARD BIBLE®, copyright© 1960, 1962, 1963, 1968, 1971, 1972, 1973, 1975, 1977, 1995 by The Lockman Foundation. Used by permission.

Scriptures marked NKJV are taken from the NEW KING JAMES VERSION (NKJV): Scripture taken from the NEW KING JAMES VERSION®. Copyright© 1982 by Thomas Nelson, Inc. Used by permission. All rights reserved.

Scriptures marked NLT are taken from the HOLY BIBLE, NEW LIVING TRANSLATION (NLT): Scriptures taken from the HOLY BIBLE, NEW LIVING TRANSLATION, Copyright© 1996, 2004, 2007 by Tyndale House Foundation. Used by permission of Tyndale House Publishers, Inc., Carol Stream, Illinois 60188. All rights reserved. Used by permission.

Scriptures marked NIV are taken from the NEW INTERNATIONAL VERSION (NIV): Scripture taken from THE HOLY BIBLE, NEW INTERNATIONAL VERSION ®. Copyright© 1973, 1978, 1984, 2011 by Biblica, Inc.™. Used by permission of Zondervan

CONTENTS

Acknowledgments   v
Foreword   ix
Acknowledgement   xiii

1. What It Looks Like   1
2. Clarity: Is This a Spiritual Parent, a Mentor, or Friend?   8
3. Let's Talk About the Parent   15
4. How Did I Get Here?   21
5. When the Answer Is No   25
6. The Mentor/The Coach/The Parent (There Is a Difference)   30
7. How Do I Feel Now? (The Blessings of Having a Spiritual Parent)   35
8. (What We Are Dealing With) The Orphan Spirit   39
9. Prayer   48

About the Author   51

ACKNOWLEDGMENTS

∽

Foremost I acknowledge my Lord and Savior Jesus Christ. The master teacher, the lover of my soul. Jesus is the Author and Finisher of all that concerns me.

∽

To my husband, Fred "BOO" that always has my back. This man is phenomenal.

∽

To my children you have made such a sacrifice to share me with others, I love you and I thank you.

∽

Special thanks to our ministerial team that is always hungry for more of the Word of God, and pushes for deeper understanding, and finally to those that encourage me to rest. I am thankful for those who know to diligently keep to their assignment of prayer for me. I thank you, so very much for every sacrifice.

∼

To my publisher, Pastor Angela, owner "Forward Write Now Publishing" and her team.

∼

To those great men and women, I have mentored, covered spiritually in guidance and restoration, corrected, and have remained so close in many ways. Those true sons and daughters that call me "Ma" and know for certain that I am the voice they are hearing to lead them into greater things so that spiritual multiplication continues in the earth. As the word describes in **Genesis 9:7** (NLT) *"Now you must have many children and repopulate the earth. Yes, multiply and fill the earth."* At the end of each chapter, you will find transformational life experiences from some who call me their spiritual mother, mentor or coach.

∼

These below that have so timely poured into me in different areas and our relationships are meaningful.
    Dale and Barbara Wentroble

Dr. Mark Hanby
Bishop GG Bloomer
Apostle Axel Sippach
Dr. Paul Gaehrig
Apostle Patricia Tyous

In this writing, I hope to bring clarity to help you identify who your spiritual parents are, how to distinguish who the mentors are, and who the coaches are in your life. This writing is not for everyone. Specifically, it is for those who have been in church most of their lives and are seeking the new and a change.

Spiritual parents, I pray this will help you better understand what you are called to do. Mentors, or coaches I pray that you will become aware of the boundaries that need to be in place. I pray for each of you, that you will do your assignments greatly and continue to empower those you are called to serve.

FOREWORD

～

An orphan spirit! A fatherless generation! How often we hear those phrases. How little we understand the dynamics involved in these painful situations.

God is often called Father in the Bible. Jesus usually addressed God as Father. Jesus needed affirmation from His Father to fulfill His assignment on the earth. Therefore, when Jesus was baptized in the river Jordan, the heavens opened, and a voice was released from Father God. "...*Thou art My beloved Son, in Thee I am well-pleased.*" **Luke 3:22b** (KJV) Father God affirmed His love and relationship with Jesus. The Son was now able to fulfill His destiny on Earth.

The relationship between Father God and Jesus sets the example of the family God wants in the Earth. His determination is to have families. The first institution God established in the earth was family. God's plan for a family was that it would be a place of covenant relationships. Family members would love one another, strengthen one another and walk together to fulfill God's purposes in the Earth. God desired sons that would look like Him and do the same things he did. These sons find their origin at the beginning of the earth before the Fall of Adam and Eve. When I refer to sons, these individuals should be understood as children of God without gender. These sons were to be co-laborers with Father God. They would transform every sphere of society and cause Earth to look more like heaven.

However, the plan of God for sons to look like Father and to perform God's intention does not always happen. Many believers have never received the healing power of God from the wounds of fatherlessness. They have never received the affirmation from an earthly father to let them know that the father loves them and is pleased with them. Therefore, destiny may be hindered or never come to fulfillment.

Not only does the individual suffer due to fatherlessness but the earth also suffers. Violence, murder, trafficking, poverty, famine, disease and myriads of other difficulties plague the Earth and its inhabitants. The earth groans for the manifest sons of God to arise and bring transformation into the earth. *"For this anxious longing of the creation waits eagerly for the revealing of the sons of God."* **Romans 8:19** (NASB)

Yet, God is the God of all hope! He can restore what has been lost in a believer's life. He can even heal and restore fatherlessness and break the power of an orphan spirit. God has placed spiritual fathers, spiritual parents, and spiritual families in the Body of Christ. These loving individuals can love, heal, equip and affirm spiritual sons. They can take the least likely person and restore them to the original intent of Father God.

Dr. Shirley Brown is an example of a spiritual parent with a proven track for spiritual parenting. Her book will help believers break out of an old season of abandonment, hopelessness, and failure. The book opens a way for believers to discover their true identity, purpose, and destiny for their lives. We are living in a prophetic season that promises to break the curse of fatherlessness. *"And he shall turn the heart of the fathers to the children, and the heart of the children to their fathers, lest I come and smite the earth with a curse."* **Malachi 4:6** (KJV)

Get ready for a new journey from where you are to where God intends for you to be. Your life and your walk with Father God will never be the same after you implement principles found in this book.

Apostle Barbara Wentroble, President
International Breakthrough Ministries
Breakthrough Business leaders
www.barbarawentroble.com

ACKNOWLEDGEMENT

∾

This book will bless every reader. There are multiple dimensions of the parent-child relationship that God teaches through the Bible to benefit believers. However, many lessons will come from living it out in relationships with others. While most people want to hear from the Lord only through dramatic signs, and wonders, God gives multiple examples through the Word of help from kind acts through men and women of God filled with wisdom, knowledge, the love of Christ, and compassion for someone else's situation–Spiritual Parents.

We must be cautious of the tricks of the adversary that will draw people into isolation when they need to be seeking direction. *"The way of a fool is right in his own eyes, but a wise man is he who listens to counsel."* **Proverbs 12:15** (KJV)

This book by Dr. Shirley Brown will give readers clarity and establish roles in spiritual parenting within these chosen blessed relationships. Whether serving as a spiritual parent to others, or as a person needing holy guidance, there is wisdom in this powerful book to turn situations around.

Imagine a world where confused people achieve understanding through fruitful conversations, or when a person hears someone speak life over their future and then actually walk with them into the promises of God. The possibilities are endless within a godly relationship with spiritual parents. *"He whose ear listens to the life-giving reproof will dwell among the wise. He who neglects discipline despises himself, but he who listens to reproof acquires understanding. The fear of the LORD is the instruction for wisdom, and before honor comes humility."* **Proverbs 15:31-33** (NASB)

As one standing in the office of an Apostle, the hope that comes with having such a tool for the people of God's kingdom —as this book will prove to be—is a welcomed delight. May God bless and edify those who are seeking a spiritual parent, and every spiritual parent who reads this book.

Apostle J Q Lockett
Grace Church of Stone Mountain
1028 Second Street
Stone Mountain, GA 30083
Gracechurchstmtn@gmail.com

1
WHAT IT LOOKS LIKE

∽

Those entry and exit places are for purposes of wisdom which could only be for a season and others for development of character. Some entries are there for a mantle to be released; Some destinies can never be released until we come into the company of that person He ordained to show up in our life. It is as though we understand that more is required but how? Then this spiritual giant of wisdom and encouragement walks into our life and we begin the journey.

Perhaps you are so fragile so there can't be many voices speaking in your life to guide or direct. Otherwise, confusion comes; chaos comes; bewilderment comes; which in turns brings delay. So, important to be careful who you allow to walk in and out of your life. This person determines your future this person will give life or death.

Too many people have taken on the false assumption of purpose in individuals lives and has caused multiple chaotic situations. Where does this really come from? Where does this really come from? Is it true spiritual parenting? Is it mentoring, is it friendship, Is it an unmet need? In the upcoming pages, I will explain and clarify the role of spiritual parenting, which is so needed in the body of Christ. You may ask why is it needed?

Spiritual parenting is imperative to the support, encouragement, upbuilding, and promotion of love among those within the body of Christ. Genuine spiritual parenting brings the work of His Kingdom to earth.

"Thy kingdom come, Thy will be done in earth, as it is in heaven."
Matthew 6:10 (KJV)

Correct spiritual parenting leaves us to understand the process of legacy. Legacy will produce fruit; it is a multiplication process. You will be remembered for your contribution to the earth. In the natural, we were created to multiply upon the earth. Spiritually, we do so with direction, guidance, and birthing. As an instruction is given, it will either catapult us into destiny or send us into exile. Remember Adam and Eve. The voice of God was there giving them complete instruction, but another voice seeped in and they missed it.

As spiritual parents, we have this opportunity again to make a difference. So, we go forth again with voices released in the land to move His called ones those that are evangelists, prophets, teachers, apostles, pastors, and other equipping gifts in the Body of Christ forward. Learning spiritual truths come from that person that the Lord has allowed in our lives. A reminder this person recognizes the gift in you. It will be a lasting relationship.

Spiritual parents, you have a key role in all of this. That we exhibit ourselves as examples for others not that those following become slaves unto us. As we have developed our relationship with the Father it is now time that we teach others to develop a relationship and begin to exhibit the characteristics of their Father.

Pay close attention to **1 Thessalonians 3:1-13** (NIV).

"So, when we could stand it no longer, we thought it best to be left by ourselves in Athens. We sent Timothy, who is our brother and co-worker in God's service in spreading the gospel of Christ, to strengthen and encourage you in your faith, so that no one would be unsettled by these trials. For you know quite well that we are destined for them. In fact, when we were with you, we kept telling you that we would be persecuted. And it turned out that way, as you well know. For this reason, when I could stand it no longer, I sent to find out about your faith. I was afraid that in some way the tempter had tempted you and that our labors might have been in vain.

Timothy's Encouraging Report
But Timothy has just now come to us from you and has brought good news about your faith and love. He has told us that you always have pleasant memories of us and that you long to see us, just as we also long to see you. Therefore, brothers and sisters, in all our distress and persecution we were encouraged about you because of your faith. For now, we really live, since you are standing firm in the Lord. How can we thank God enough for you in return for all the joy we have in the presence of our God because

> *of you? Night and day we pray most earnestly that we may see you again and supply what is lacking in your faith. Now may our God and Father himself and our Lord Jesus clear the way for us to come to you. May the Lord make your love increase and overflow for each other and for everyone else, just as ours does for you. May he strengthen your hearts so that you will be blameless and holy in the presence of our God and Father when our Lord Jesus comes with all his holy ones."*

Spiritual parenting is all about nurturing an individual. These parents are called and graced to do what they do, it simply means they are already designed to handle the assignment given to them. They are built to carry this type of weight; they will not get not angry quick, they will not ignore their responsibilities and will always protect, develop and love. It is a connection that brings growth with fruitful maturity.

> *"For if you were to have countless tutors in Christ, yet you would not have, many fathers, for in Christ Jesus I became your father through the gospel." 1 Corinthians 4:15 (NASB)*

A newborn requires an extra amount of adult attention. Spiritually as the child matures, they can move forward to be in groups for more understanding, but firm instruction must be given. This parent is responsible for discipline, discipling, and delivery. They are always there with the child no matter where they are there throughout the process.

Now we shift to others that are called into our life for growth. Those that step in for different reasons. The mentor steps in for a moment and works with the individual on a specific task. They hold a temporary spot at times. They are never forgotten they are assigned for specific tasks. It can be in finances, business plans, preparation for a new job and so much more. Their assignment is very specific.

This writing is not gender based men need mothering also; Fathering is being restored back to the body of Christ. It is being restored by freedom of worship, having relationships, creating safe environments. We are coming to the place to say that it is not a fatherless generation. Things are changing so a generation will come forth exhibiting a New Testament church with believers exhibiting the work of the Father. The sons will manifest!

"For the creation waits in eager expectation for the children of God to be revealed." **Romans 8:19** *(NIV)*

Pastors Dimitri and Valerie Rayner
Leaders Destiny International Ministries

In the beginning of my walk with Christ, I never knew there was such a thing as a spiritual parent. I always thought spiritual parents were just pastors and members. Your hope was to be liked enough that someone would teach you by example the Biblical principles necessary for this walk. Since being at Destiny International Ministries, Apostle Brown has been what I never knew existed.

A natural mother takes care of the child by loving them, feeding and clothing the child and so much more. The mother teaches the child how to treat others in such a way that they would someday repeat the process and show the same love to others. Apostle Brown is doing the same but on a spiritual level. I have experienced this in my own personal transformation. She loves through the love of Christ and feeds her congregation the Word, so it can be digested and understood. She clothes her spiritual children in the truth of what the Word says about us. She teaches us so that we not only have a prosperous walk in Christ but that we can teach others that they too may have a prosperous walk.

This spiritual parenting is bringing forth a legacy that can be passed down generation to generation.

Pastor Dimitri

Everything around me was sinking. I was surrounded by people, yet I felt all alone. Was God speaking then, I honestly wouldn't have known His voice to discern it. I needed guidance, clarity, and direction at a level that was unknown to me, none seemed to understand, including my own birth parents. True spiritual parenting is just like the natural, but even the more because your very soul is at stake and if in the wrong hands, your life as well. Truthfully, I didn't know that I needed a spiritual mother until I had one. As a grown woman and mother who dealt with my own "momma issues" the last thing I felt I needed was a mom.

However a spiritual Mother was what I needed, and her entrance came right before what was almost my death. Apostle's entry wasn't a "takeover" in any type of way. In my personal testimony, I speak truth in saying that God sent an angel to bring me out of where I was, which was a very dark place in life and dropped me off at her church's doorstep which was a safe place. Apostle Brown came in and did the one thing that won me over, she loved me. Sounds so cliché I know, but that was it. There was no judgment, no bashing, no questions asked, she just loved me. She loved me to where I had to trust her. I didn't even trust God. A true spiritual parent doesn't stop there, she then pointed me back to Christ, back to my first love. She never took the credit and never let me forget not only who I was but who HE was. My parents and my spiritual parents are both respected and loved honored and know their place in my life. A spiritual parent doesn't replace the natural parent, they are a bonus. They direct, lead, teach, correct, discipline, plant and when done properly, they can watch that seed grow and blossom into good fruit which continues to produce more fruit. If not for this gift in the person of Apostle Brown, I would not be the mother, wife, leader, or even daughter that I am today.

Pastor Val "Songbird" Rayner

2
CLARITY: IS THIS A SPIRITUAL PARENT, A MENTOR, OR FRIEND?

∽

We must have a firm understanding of the role of individuals in our life. That understanding produces fruit and brings us into maturity and can cause death.

A mentor is wise and can guide you through a particular event. The mentor can lead you through events. You can have several mentors at one time, for example, one who has an expertise in finances – that one will develop budgeting, etc. A mentor helps you develop trust in individuals, so they can have positive role models to see how to accomplish a task. Most mentors are seasonal. Let's classify them as an aide that develop us. Mentors can be accountability partners, they want to make sure you are accomplishing what has been set out to do. They have a plan in place, normally you walk a timeline. Mentors are usually classified as teachers they bring structure to the rough edges. Mentors are life givers when you feel like you can't go on they design a way to keep you moving.

A spiritual parent knows your calling; the one that stands by you through thick and thin. When you fall they are there to pick you up; they are protectors. They lead you into sonship This doesn't mean you are necessarily in their ministry forever. There is a bond that always points you to Jesus. With the spiritual parent, there are birthing times and with that, it is an equipping and sending for the child. They walk this spiritual journey with you all the way. They impart wisdom, order, knowledge, and understanding. You may not always agree with your spiritual parent. They can't give you a yes for everything. They do not always agree with you what you desire remember they have been granted supernatural gifting to see farther than you. They are to make sure that you are not dropped in this process. Spiritual parents are like natural parents they will keep a natural eye on you always. You may not get a yes for everything and that is a good thing. You are to be held accountable, even if you move on to your own ministry or to another ministry, there is a bond and a level of respect for one another. You may not get everything from that spiritual parent you may need developing in other areas that the parent can't perfect in you. Always keep your trust in God and He will perfect all. They are not dictating, controlling, or overbearing. If so, they aren't parenting correctly. The spiritual parent is readily available. You can't call someone your spiritual parent and you have no access to them. There will be a divine connection with this parent. You will feel the love and you will know this is a godsend. It won't be arguments it will be experiences of great joy although you may not have a yes to everything. It will be times of grand spiritual revelation. They will give you an opportunity to error and stumble but provide you with a safe environment to do so without judgment. Many have ruined vital relationships with their spiritual Fathers/Mothers because of a misunderstanding of why they were in their lives.

There must be a complete understanding of who and why that person is in your life. Without that clarity, you will never develop properly. You can subconsciously walk in disobedience instead of obedience. You must understand who that person is if not you will develop with a spirit of rejection, a spirit of pride, and possibly even developing an orphan spirit. Each spirit pull us into delay. After delaying other attachments come with it. I did a message on the five kings in the cave. Joshua 10. These kings represent the heart issues. They were in the cave surviving while the army was out fighting. The little things (demons) were addressed but the big conceived thing was still hidden deep in the heart. The kings in the cave had been hiding but it was time to pull them out and bring them to submission so others could come to release freedom. You must have a focus on freedom. Reminder: you are a multiplier.

As we look at spiritual parenting, we use buzz words such as covering, in any way not to discredit anyone but clarity must be bought to words, so people can develop properly and not be held in a spiritual web. A spiritual web is a place of seeing a thing but unable to reach it, you are stuck; something has grabbed ahold of you and it won't allow you to move freely. Bouncing here and there and not knowing who they are. Spiritual Covering simply mean there is usually someone you submit your ministry to. They collaborate with you in ministry decision making. I believe that biblically we should look at covenant relationship instead of spiritual covering. We should at least understand what we have become a part of. The covenant is that we are in agreement and this is sealed. Why are you connected to this organization or individual? Are they pushing me forward or am I assisting only to bankroll an individual or organization that knows nothing about me? In parenting, mentoring, or covering (covenant relations) a key thing must be known the individuals are not yours. They are in your care and you serve them for growth and development. In doing so you must be ready to release them to go forth, you can't hold them. They have an assignment also! We must know one another let the mentor do their part and the spiritual parent never be threatened.

Sometimes the spiritual parent can work with the mentor all to get you to the place you should be. You must always seek the wisdom of the Lord and ask questions like "where I am right now?" "what do I need?". Always walk in obedience don't get frustrated and walk away from the very thing that is designed for you to achieve high levels.

There are things to keep in mind when looking for a mentor, that you can also do when you are seeking a spiritual parent. For example, you are investigating personality, you take an active role you determine what you need. This is difficult to do for a spiritual parent it is just a knowing that this is the person and the person will know also. This parent labors in prayer to see the next move for you. Their yes is yes and no is no. They are firm but supportive.

Research must have taken place when looking for a good mentor. That good mentor possesses excellent communication skills and can adjust to the personality type to communicate what is needed. Even being a mentee, you are challenged to accomplish what you have set before the mentor and again you may not be happy all the time. It is stretching you, so some things will be uncomfortable in the stretch and press.

In this whole process, there is hope there will be no domination or manipulation from the parent. They desire you to soar beyond your wildest dreams. We also consider friends in the equation of the spiritual parent, mentor, coach. When we think of friends, we can lose perspective in our thoughts. A friend just accepts you the way you are they don't change you, "it is an I like you and you like me situation", you stand in a mutual agreement. You enjoy one another. Friendships develop over time by spending time together. Friends have common interests, they go to movies, try out new things together, take trips together, etc.

Can a mentor become a friend possibility but rarely accepted? You don't want to make that mistake of trying to develop a friendship with a mentor or spiritual parent. Let me be very clear I am not saying that you cannot be friends I am making a distinction between the mentor and a friendship. If a friendship develops then that is wonderful never go into the relationship wanting it to be a friendship. Know what is needed when you go into any relationship. No one wants any hurt or disappointment. Mentors are assignment driven and with that in mind, there is really no time for extra curriculum activities. A true friend can be there and we must realize that the mentor may not always be able to be in place. Learn to accept the difference in the relationships, keep a communication line open.

*"A man of many companions may come to ruin, but there is a friend sticks closer than a brother ." **Proverbs 18:24** (NIV)*

Elder Cynthia O. Bernard
Elder and Dean of Education
Destiny International Ministries

When the angel came to visit Mary, the mother of Jesus, and delivered the message of what was about to happen, the power of the Holy Spirit would overshadow her, and the child she would carry was from God. The birthing of a spiritual son or daughter is perplexing and along the same lines. God orchestrates the circumstances for the birthing.

We don't choose our parent in the natural and neither can we choose them in the spirit, but we know them by the Spirit. The voice of a spiritual parent is known of by their child and there is a response (There are times the hearing of spiritual son /daughter can take a minute). Our ears are in tune to hear truth and wisdom, hearts are longing for direction, encouragement and a place of refuge and rest. The teaching of the parent gives strength and confidence to move forward in the right direction. Their voice of correction reminds us of the Father's love and when we don't agree they don't change, they love us through those rough moments never letting us go, they understand we are a part of them, and the assignment must be completed. For me, understanding the role of a spiritual parent took a moment, there was a process of heart connecting our hearts mine to hers and hers to mine and because Apostle is who she is, she did not waver nor let me stop her from being who she is. Apostle patiently waited for me to stop running not physically but in my heart. Once I was settled, there was a demand placed on my gift was not more than I could handle but enough to get me up, strategic and effective. There were moments I *wanted to give up and run hoping she would run behind me and she simply explained, "you have to stand, I cannot carry you not any further I'm behind you but from here you have to walk and trust the God in you" (this memory brings me to tears, because she was so right, I had to stand). The demand called me to a higher place in Christ, relying on God and supported by her. Watching her navigate through ministry and the grace of how she loved other sons and daughter helped to make my footing sure, her transparency made her a safe refuge, her place of ministry and life lessons have helped to transform my life always pointing me to Christ. I still have a way to go. I am still developing but I am on my way. Thank you, Apostle, for being you and allowing me to be me.*

3

LET'S TALK ABOUT THE PARENT

∼

A parent is a caregiver, I would like to make a comparison between a parent and a wolf. Parents are caring and not devouring. Parents see afar and are not lurking. Parents are giving and not always in need. Parents are respectful, parents are considerate, parents are understanding. Wolves are manipulative, devouring, cunning, and territorial. Remember that a wolf's real personality is often hidden under the character of his or her social position, aggressive, and friendly with the ability to make strong emotional attachments. This is an example to safeguard you when you are looking for that parent.

When you look at this, you can determine if this is a good relationship. All parents are not emotionally stable. There are things to look at in the parent, their character, their connections, are they submitted to someone, do they have any spiritual children, how are they developed. No one is perfect but you want to see this person as productive not hot-tempered, willing to serve, compassionate. You must be watchful that you are not malnourished. Everyone can't eat the same food. Some can't eat junk food, a lot of us need well-balanced meals. What we eat shows our development, look at it like this, if all you take in is carbs you will be overweight and may face some health challenges. If you are a well-balanced eater you will be physically fit with exercise. Just like in the natural – you can't eat too many carbs, or all fried food, eat too much of it and you become sluggish. It is the same way spiritual not having a balanced diet will cause you to be off in prophecy, interpretation of scriptures, discernment and more.

Some people we are desiring to be our spiritual parents have not been healed (spiritually) yet. If you push your way into the den of an unhealthy leader to be a parent could be devastating. Integrity must be the high quality that spiritual parent possesses, they are examples. As I have said individuals are not perfect but transparent with healing. You never want to connect to someone that has unmet needs, they are insecure, they are paranoid of others and much more. This will be an open door to trauma and constant misunderstanding for both of you.

A spiritual parent will be God appointed and not self-appointed. Now I would like to share an experience I had in my early ministry. I moved to North Carolina in 1989 and served a great ministry faithfully for over 13 years in many capacities. That is where my leader saw a greater potential in me and insisted for me to start ministerial training. My aim was to just tell people about Jesus and see them set free without all the rest of the training and all the frills. During my time of service, the Holy Spirit spoke to me that He was preparing me for more. I was very reluctant to obey the voice of the Lord because I was satisfied where I was, but my assignment was bigger than what I could see. I moved from that local ministry to an international ministry again the leader sees some more potential in me. I submitted myself and was obedient not to delay anything new no matter what, I was focused ready to receive instructions for my next spiritual level. It wasn't about me getting a position but being in position for my next appointment by God. By being obedient I was released to move forward to pastor. I was on time for services when asked to do something I was in place, I was not debatable with my leader, I adhered to the word of God I applied **Hebrews 13:17** (KJV) *"Obey them that have the rule over you, and submit yourselves: for they watch for your soul, as they that must give account, that they may do it with joy, and not with grief: for that is unprofitable for you."*

Today we are a flourishing ministry training, equipping and sending individuals purposefully into their Destiny. These parents carry keys that will move you forward. They are individuals that are not competitors with you. They celebrate you when you teach, preach better than them. The parents help you break cycles in your life, they get to the root cause why a situation repeats itself. These cycles can be in finances, relationships, etc. anything that holds you back.

A spiritual parent is appointed of God. Remember, they are in place to get you to your destiny. Their goal is for you to be whole in all areas of life. We cannot have multiple spiritual parents, we can have many mentors, coaches but not parents. The parent must be careful not to become so comfortable in this that they will want to help everyone, taking on situations that they are not called to. If they do they will attract opportunists. They just get what they need and move on. Let it be clear that you are not assigned to everyone just because your heart breaks for them

> Study 1 **Corinthians 4:15** - *"Even if you had ten thousand guardians in Christ, you do not have many fathers, for in Christ Jesus I became your father through the gospel."*

This scripture will give you understanding to acknowledge who holds the role of spiritual parent, mentor or coach.

Overseer Clarence "Ronnie"
Elder at Destiny International Ministries
Overseer of No-Nonsense Kingdom Alliance (NNKA) and
Dionne Green, Administrator
Destiny International Ministries
No-Nonsense Kingdom Alliance (NNKA)

Previously, Dionne and I have been very fortunate to have my mother, Daisy Burgess, to fill the role as a spiritual mother in our lives. During her life, she always took time to mentor and pour her insight into many pastors, elders and other leaders that sought to please God. Unsurprisingly, one she shared with before her transition to being with God is Apostle Shirley R. Brown. My wife and I believe the relationship with Apostle Brown was preparing us for not only a spiritual leader but a spiritual mother who would speak life to us.

As we thought on how to write this transformational life experience on spiritual parenting my wife, Dionne saw a vision of a lighthouse. "A lighthouse symbolizes a way forward and a way to navigate through rough waters of life. The lighthouse illustrates concepts such as danger, risk, adversity, challenge, and vigilance. Lighthouses symbolize the way forward and help in navigating our way through rough waters whether those waters be financial, personal, business or spiritual in nature." (Quote and explanation from the website (www.johnlund.com)) The lighthouse is a symbol of spiritual strength and emotional guidance which Apostle Brown has provided to us as our spiritual mother.

The Book of Titus gives a brief glimpse of the importance of this role in the church, with Paul instructing Timothy to ask older women to give instruction /or teach in the lives of their younger counterparts. Both men and women need spiritual mothers. "The older women likewise, that they be reverent in behavior, not slanderers, not given too much wine, teachers of good things -- that they admonish the young women to love their husbands, to love their children, to be discreet, chaste, homemakers, good, obedient to their husbands, that the word of God may not be blasphemed." **Titus 2:3-4** *(NKJV)*

As our spiritual mother, Apostle Shirley R. Brown is all that a believer could ask for in a spiritual mother. She provides practical instruction and wisdom we can apply to our everyday life. Ma Apostle covers us in prayer and seeks the face of God on our behalf. She has the God-given insight to speak into areas of our lives. Sometimes it can be uncomfortable. Her counseling has helped us navigate through some of the roughest waters of our lives and marriage. She loves us as if she has given birth to us. Her most significant influence on us is her unwavering faith through tough circumstances that would leave the average believer questioning God.

Apostle Brown is an honorable example to all her spiritual children whom God assigned her to mother. As our spiritual mother she mentors imparts Christian character, gives correction, motivates, encourages, her tutelage gives us reasonability, disciplined lives. For that Dionne and I are eternally grateful.

It is an honor and blessing to write this life-transitional moment on being prepared for our spiritual mother and as it states in **Proverbs 31:28** *(NLT), "Her children stand and bless her. Her husband praises."*

4

HOW DID I GET HERE?

∼

In our modern-day society our lives are filled with one activity to another we are constantly trying to find. We are trying to figure out how we got to a certain point when our intention was something else.

How did you get to the point of busyness instead of accomplishing what the Lord said? You can get overly attracted to the individual instead of the call. You looked at the individual instead of seeing that the person was sent to you for your development; assisting you into maturity.

There can be times you look back and wonder endlessly how I did I arrive at this point. Most of those points are frustration, aggravation, misunderstandings, all moving you out of your destined place. Often, you are moving seeking someone's approval that leads you in performance mode and not God's will. People's approval should never be your desire. When one is in this state of mind it can cause performance driven activities that take you totally from the assigned purpose. This state can cause a lot of misunderstandings. You can wind up missing the very person intended to lead you into greater overstepping your boundaries causing aggravation from the mentor or spiritual parent, this is like a double whammy causing both to miss it. Some other areas that can be affected are your relationships, finances, health, and future. Your spiritual parent wants you to be unbroken, in an undamaged state, not one part of you but all of you.

This spiritual parent has been somewhat twisted and perverted, the appearance is controlling, ungodly bonding what could have been the reason so much overcompensation for acceptance. We are learning in these writings something different. The parent is to demonstrate encouragement, empowerment, and understanding. They are to get you to your there. You may ask why do I need someone to lead me spiritually? The reason is that they want you to deepen your relationship with God. It is called spiritual maturing which develops exponential growth. Receiving guidance is like learning to walk. A baby isn't born walking, the baby goes through many stages before walking. One day the baby stands, stabilizes and no longer falls, no longer is afraid and starts its new journey of walking. You must want it from your heart and not from a place of performing, you must learn how to accept it how it comes. Learn to relax and stop being frustrated. Take your levels of success and be thankful. Trust God to provide everything that is needed, He is the ultimate provider of everything even relationships. We now can understand the purpose of spiritual parents better. You must want this process it can be very trying to experience, but it is well worth it. It trains you in great relationship principles. Principles such as respect, transparency, non-judgmental, trust, empowerment. Principles that will stick when nothing else endures.

It will take you through the rough seasons and you will say no more "How did I get to this point". Have an ear to hear, a heart to submit and endure.

"Submit to God and be at peace with him; in this way, prosperity will come to you. Accept instruction from his mouth and lay up his words in your heart." Job 22:21-22 (NIV)

Ursula Jacobs Williams
Executive Pastor
Destiny International Ministries

For years I was in a relationship with an individual I looked to as my spiritual parent, but it was a situation that was not favorable or healthy. But it was what I was birthed into and what I knew. I worked diligently in ministry, serving many, and just performing, performing, performing. I spent so much time pleasing everyone else that I didn't know who I was and neglecting my own self-worth. I wasn't happy, wasn't serving God with joy but with dread and I was guilty of wearing a "church" mask. Often I asked myself "what in the world am I doing here and how can I get out?"

Then, there came a day when I said: "I am done with church and crazy pastors." I made up my mind no more church attendance for me. I understand now that God had other plans. I always say

He set me up and guided me right to the place He wanted me. Ok, now I'm in a new place asking myself "how did I get here?" This new place was different. The people were different, the atmosphere was different and most important the leader was different. God had actually placed me in the life of someone that saw my value and made me see it also. She poured into me and pulled out of me of me all that God had invested. Wait, was I being told that I could serve God without constraints, without crazy demands and I could actually live a life with balance and be happy? YES! No more performance, pretense or church mask! A true relationship with God was on the horizon.

Jeremiah 29:11 *(KJV) states "For I know the thoughts that I think toward you, saith the Lord, thoughts of peace, and not of evil, to give you an expected end." God had a plan, I was part of the plan now and so was my spiritual parent. I didn't always believe that but I had to learn it! He had a plan and He had a person assigned to my life to help carry out the plan. I had to first learn that God loved me and wasn't out to punish me but wanted to bless me beyond my wildest imagination. I had to learn to accept His love for me before I could accept the love of another person.*

Through many trying times and layers of healing, the day I realized my true spiritual parent was the day I heard these words spoken directly "I am here to serve you". WOW, those six words carried so much weight and would change my life forever. No more would I have to ask, "how did I get here?" I now know how I got here!

5

WHEN THE ANSWER IS NO

There are times when the parent must say "no" and in this chapter we will understand the no process. You may even find some repetitive thoughts. It is purposefully to get you to understand that the NO is not to destroy you but to build you up. That parent is always strong even in their worst situations for they are relying on the Holy Spirit also teaching spiritual children the same. The parents do not stroke egos. They look like natural parents as far as relationship skills. They nurture in this you are in a safe environment that produces normal growth. Assurance is there but a push must be in place. A hand in the back, encouraging you to try to new things. Reminder: it is directional but not your direction it is the direction in which God wants you to go. Honor and respect are always given but have a watchful eye if everything turns to the parent that may not be the right person. Spiritual parents help individuals see the potential in themselves, they help identify spiritual gifts and they also identify habits which need to be broken. This is a sharing position of service. The parent must be transparent, and the child does also, nothing about this is one-sided. Parents teach their children intentionally and unintentionally. Spiritual parents, you have much wisdom, to give. This will allow those in your presence to have a different perspective on things. Be transparent! The meaning of transparent is clear, see-through.

We have had enough cover-up in ministry. Let's see clearly so we can see greater works coming forth. Wisdom is not only shared but impartation is a must, vision is imparted. Spiritual parents help you see your own success. They don't demise what your assignment is they come alongside and pray you to that place. A true spiritual parent never takes your assignment and change it to what they want. They hear your heart and begin in prayer for direction on how to lead you properly. It is vital that we get the right downloads from heaven to move the assignment.

They teach you how to walk it out. Spiritual parents come to give you balance so many can't find balance, but that parent can show you places of balance like no one else. Remember they have been there. Now, mentors, coaches can give you a plan and hold you accountable for balance. The decision would come from the individual if they desired mentor, coach, or spiritual parent. They teach you how to talk, spiritual parents model your speech. You don't need to react to everything so quickly. You know when to speak and when not to speak. You understand the timing of reactions. Your discernment becomes sharpen, no longer foggy and you may use that gift.

The "no" you receive from the spiritual parent is not to manipulate nor dominate you. The no is for correction and it could be a challenge, there are even times that a no can be for confrontation. We must understand the voice of the parent, after all, it is a partner with the voice of the Lord. Take no fear you will know if the person is to be in your life. A leader is good only if they let others become responsible for themselves. Like babies learning to walk the parent stands the baby and days come on and there is no holding, no pulling...the principle is the same for the spiritual parent let them go and call them into their future.

Apostle Kimberly Armstrong
Senior Pastor
Mount Zion Church of Deliverance Ministries

For nearly ten years, I had no suitable relationship with anyone that I could call a spiritual mother. I sought the Lord for one, but nothing ever seemed to work in my favor. God would say No, every time. I often wondered, why did that keep happening repeatedly. When searching for someone I thought was spiritually sound; seasoned enough to help guide me spiritually, dealt with disappointment after disappointment. God continued to say "no" and imposters continued to show up. I had many trying to fulfill the role of being my spiritual parent. However, they never went through the birthing process. They recognized the gift and call on my life, but they were not spiritually equipped to help me with my assignment. I had many questions racing through my mind. I said

Lord, "they are anointed, they've been with you for years and even have thriving ministries but why isn't there any evidence of a true connection. I later discovered there was a connection, but it was not a divine one.

For over the course of about 15 or more years, I faced much heartache and disappointment. Each time I met a leader I'd think to myself, this person must be the one. God would reveal the true heart of the person, and it left me wounded and causing me to move on. While I'm thinking this was God's yes for me, in all actuality it wasn't. It was God's no. I took a while, but I finally learned that when God gave me the answer of "no", it was my yes. You may ask "how did I reach that conclusion?" Well, it wasn't an easy journey. After many failed attempts of misunderstanding the process, I came to understand and accept the language of God and His Kingdom. Everything that I went through, was only spiritually developing me. **Romans 8:28** (KJV) says, "And we know that all things work together for good to them that love God, to them who are the called according to his purpose."

Years of going through a process unknown to me, only prepared me for the YES that God was leading me too. Eventually, the day came God sent me my spiritual parent. The gift in this person He had purposed and designed just for me. Guess what? The gift came with the ability to say "No." However, it was a no that came from a Godly place. I cannot say I like it when my spiritual parent says "No," especially when it involves something I really want to do. But I'm willing to accept it because it's for my good.

Remember, spiritual parents will say no. They are God's agents watching over your soul. I now have a yes from God and my spirit says "Yes" thankful that God said No when I wanted my way so badly. It hurt me, but it made me stronger and prepared me for my

*Greater, my Now, and my Next. King David picked it up in **Psalms 119:71** (KJV) saying, "It is good for me that I have been afflicted; that I might learn thy statutes." So even when God says "No" to what you thought was your yes, hang in there. He will guide you to His YES and you will be glad He did. Wait on Him.*

6

THE MENTOR/THE COACH/THE PARENT (THERE IS A DIFFERENCE)

∼

Mentors provide instruction and they assist to help you to navigate through difficult seasons in life. Specifically targeting an area that needs wisdom with maturity. They design well thought out plans that will allow you to escape a present dilemma. They are seasonal. Those that have misplaced their relationship with mentors and allow them to fill roles as pastors or spiritual parents.

The mentors also may not be as clear as to how they are relating to individuals. I often say to individuals that come into my life, "How do you perceive me?" This eliminates any confusion. I am a certified life coach, I am a mentor, a certified counselor and I am an ordained minister so, if I don't put myself in a category you will relate to me as you see me.

The parent part takes time to see if it is to come through

prayer. I have had many people come and say I am their spiritual mother and as soon as I say "no" about a situation they have determined I am no longer that spiritual parent. My question is how you feel about your natural parent. The parent is a permanent voice. It crucial to understand the mentoring process so you are not dealing with unmet needs and emotional instability. The mentor can develop skills, empower you to make choices, develop life skills. They are trusted to answer open-ended questions. This is not a spiritual parent and possibly not the permanent voice. It is key we understand relationships, how they develop and what they mean. I always say understand your relationship with Jesus Christ, and His grand relationship with us, once that happens we can value those that are placed in our lives. These individuals are providing time, commitment, resources (financial, materials), and positioning all strategically poured in our lives. Coaching aims to improve performance. Coaches focus on the now! *"Coaching is unlocking a person's potential to maximize their own performance. It is helping them to learn rather than teaching them."* John Whitmore

The spiritual parent will laugh with you, cry with you, be transparent with you. Never allow what is shared or seen in private settings or the company of others become an excuse you mislabeled them. Your spiritual parent is human. The focus is not to become your friend or even to spend a lot of time together but to make sure your assignment is complete. Be confident of who you are in Christ.

There are times that relationships with a spiritual parent can turn to friendship, the mentor also but it is not forced it just happens. The spiritual parent creates avenues for visitations. That spiritual parent never becomes common with you or you with them. We want no vital relationships ruined, with spiritual parents, mentors, or coaches because of misunderstanding of why one is in your life.

Dr. Saundra Wall Williams
Chief Executive Officer
The Vision Building Institute

Dr. Shirley Brown: The Mentor and The Coach

In today's world of professional and personal development, many people have mentors and/or coaches. In my life, I have experienced that both are of great value and I believe that you need mentors and coaches in any area of your life where you desire to move forward. My relationship with Dr. Shirley R. Brown is an example of a successful mentor and coach relationship. She has played a tremendous role in my life and ministry development. A mentor and coach often seem to serve the same function and many people often use the terms interchangeably. There is a difference in a mentor relationship and a coaching relationship. Allow me to explain our relationship.

As a mentor, Dr. Brown has guided, taught, and counseled me from her experience as a ministry leader. I view the mentor as one who has already walked a path successfully and can now mentor you to do the same. I believe that mentors have to walk alongside their mentees and set an example. For example, when I was in Divinity School at Regent University, Dr. Brown served as my mentor in the Women in Ministry course. She guided me as I developed my own ministry. Additionally, she has literally gone through life with me for the past 25 years. My professional life, my ministry life, my personal life, and my spiritual growth have all been impacted by Dr. Brown as my mentor. She has encouraged me to trust God in difficult situations and I've seen her do the same. She has guided me in ministry as I have watched her ministry to grow. We have an Elizabeth and Mary (Luke Chapter 1) relationship. She sees what's in me and she works with me to push it out so that I can do the work God has called me to do.

As my coach, Dr. Brown guides using accountability. I actually think she was coaching before coaching became popular. It always amazes me at times that she mentors me to let me know there was a better way but allows me to discover a better way while helping me to sustain my vision, and move forward in my life, ministry or career. As my coach, she has helped me to set goals and measure my performance against those goals. During this time I began to develop the skills that made me go higher in my calling of teacher. She asked me powerful questions to draw out the abilities God has put in me. Instead of telling me what to do, Dr. Brown would ask me questions such as, "If you do not invest in you, then why would others invest in you?" Like in Mark 8:27-29, Jesus used questions to draw out the answer from His followers. Dr. Brown has helps me to clarify my vision so that I can move forward in ministry, my career, and my personal life.

Dr. Brown has the experience and expertise to mentor AND has the ability to coach. She has special and valuable gifts. Out of all the mentors and coaches I have in my personal, professional, and my ministry life I have only encountered three women who are both mentor and coach to me. Dr. Brown is that for me for ministry. I count them a blessing and it is an honor to sit at their *feet to learn and grow. These ladies have laughed with me and cried with me and have pushed me to places that I did not know existed in myself! Mentors and coaches are necessary for that firm foundation in your life.*

7

HOW DO I FEEL NOW? (THE BLESSINGS OF HAVING A SPIRITUAL PARENT)

∼

Spiritual parents through the giftings of the Holy Spirit create atmospheres of love, acceptance, and rest. Spending time with the parent you should walk away feeling energized and ready to go after that assignment; you are excited to reach all your goals. The relationship is not forced, it just happens. The spiritual parent has been tested and they are a learned individual they have submitted themselves, their gifts also they have gone through the process

They have submitted themselves as sons, understanding that sonship is not gender based. They all have spiritual parents. A thought to always remember is that you can never be a parent if you never submitted yourself to a spiritual parent. Reminder: you may try to do all this alone but there will always be frustration or irritation. The spiritual parent should emanate personal integrity and they have had a divine encounter with the Lord is evident in every occasion you have with them. Remember Paul's statement to the young Timothy,

> "You, however, know all about my teaching, my way of life, my purpose, faith, patience, love, endurance, persecutions, sufferings—what kinds of things happened to me in Antioch, Iconium, and Lystra, the persecutions I endured. Yet the Lord rescued me from all of them. In fact, everyone who wants to live a godly life in Christ Jesus will be persecuted, while evildoers and impostors will go from bad to worse, deceiving and being deceived. But as for you, continue in what you have learned and have become convinced of because you know those from whom you learned it." **2 Timothy 3:10-14** (NIV)

Becoming a spiritual parent takes time to develop don"t get excited when you see their ministry or their connections, it was a process. What you see doesn't offer you the same connection it is only a foreshadow of what can come your way and even greater but you must know how to handle yourself. Spiritual parent's life is their message, the ups, and downs, the failures, the success stories, the could haves, the what ifs, and the fire experiences. Take every advantage to sit and experience their life. Here is the section that you don't want to ignore. One of the best ways to learn is by observation. I always tell sons and daughters "at all times have a pad to take notes nuggets come quick and you want to keep them close."

Atmospheres are created by spiritual parents. These are places of freedom never control, intimidation, manipulation or domination. Those are all tricks and a place where demonic forces can take hold and cause delay. Spiritual parents help you to understand your liberty in Christ and a genuine personal relationship with the Father. Spiritual parents want you to have freedom because that exhibits the relationship with God! It removes you from the idol portrait and develops a personal true relationship with the Father. This is an area you must be extremely careful in the parent cannot make this great assignment of parenting about themselves. Make sure you as the parent can keep yourself free from baggage (carrying things that are weighing you down), insults, rejection. You never want to help someone else with personal baggage because your unmet needs will spill over and destroy someone else. An extreme caution those being parented don't make that person an idol, bring them off the pedestal you don't want to be devastated with disappointment. The blessings are many from the spiritual parent. For example, they can bring protection and sound thinking. They pray for you and have your heart and back. They will battle on your behalf. They know the strategies of spiritual warfare. Not that they take on everything that you go through, but they can perceive it and you can see how they can handle themselves in the council room of the Lord on your behalf. Areas you will witness that need close attention drawn to gossip, slander, persecution, ridicule. These teach you much in ministry, other points to keep before you is a learning tool to watch how they handle themselves in crisis. Watch them lead you into maturity. Observe your way of thinking and the change that it will produce. You will long for revelation; observe the insight and experiences the parent brings. Your study habits change your appetite changes. But you must want to change more than the spiritual parent. Go through the process don't rush it. There is great joy in this.

Pastor Kenneth and Tiffany Hampton
Destiny International Ministries

*Apostle Shirley R. Brown helped us to understand that when two people get married, they are not automatically one. (**Mark 10: 8** (NIV) "and the two shall be one flesh: so they are no longer two but one flesh."*

Our marriage and lives were likened to a rollercoaster until we were graced by the covering of our Spiritual Mother and Apostle, Shirley R. Brown. The wisdom imparted to us, allowed us to gain an appreciation for one another and caused us to work more on self rather than seek to change our spouse. The environment of love came, when we recognized our own faults, focusing on how to be better overall and not magnify each other's faults. Words are powerful, and we can create a loving atmosphere, one of safety and peace, or create one filled with hostility and chaos, with simply how we speak. We choose our words wisely and we are becoming friends and can enjoy each other as more than just husband and wife. We have been divorced and remarried. You must know who your destiny is tied to and not allow your emotions to make you miss your destiny. There is safety in the multitude of counselors, therefore don't make the mistake of not seeking wise counsel. We are living testimonies, that if you listen to wise counsel, you will be in the realm of safety and bask in love as intended by God.

8

(WHAT WE ARE DEALING WITH) THE ORPHAN SPIRIT

∽

Position is how we are placed in a season. Assignment is a particular work and or course study. Vision is the act of seeing something fulfill. Each one will move you into your destiny, but someone needs to help you; God has placed some to assist you and develop you. We must know those that are among us.

The enemy is determined to see you fail. The Lord loves us so much and the enemy is outrageously angry because we have moved to that place of the Father's heart and he has nothing anymore. He will stay on task to see everything about you fails. Remember to hold firm to the scripture *"With God all things are possible"* **Matthew 19:26** (NKJV).

Many demon attacks will come from the longing for spiritual parenting. The orphan spirit will take root which will carry a variety of spirits with itself. The orphan spirit has you always trying to please which gets you deeper and deeper into a place of acceptance. We looked for validation through our work. This parent comes along and validates you through what the Holy Spirit has revealed to them in the spirit. Only a true spiritual parent can do that because they are secure in who they are. Knowing who you are in Christ is a must.

There are many characteristics to keep your spiritual eye on the lookout for the attack of Absalom (the Absalom Spirit), rejection, low esteem, the spirit of pride, false humility and many more. We have come to a time that we must distinguish the difference between the orphan spirit and true sonship. We as parents must teach abandonment, isolation, loneliness, alienation so the true sons come forth.

We must teach deliverance and healing. We as parents must go back and teach the Father's love until that love is experience, we will have one battle after another giving the enemy leverage. We become frustrated and he is laughing at how he stopped us again. Once the Father's love is instilled, we can put in place the strategies to defeat the works of the enemy. This is the missing component understanding sonship. Some of these attacks are from trauma as early as birth. We grow throughout life with a spirit of rejection and we wind up self-sabotaging ourselves because our thought process has been attacked. Hear this statement "Everyone is not against you." It will take spiritual parents with great spiritual depth and authority to break and reverse this curse to perpetuate a generational blessing and a true manifestation of sons in the earth. Only when a person is healed of fatherlessness through the love of God is the orphan spirit broken, so they can begin entering mature sonship. Sonship (we are not speaking of gender) is so important it is the future. *"For all creation is waiting eagerly for that future day when*

God will reveal who his children are." **Roman 8:19** (NLT) The earth is waiting on you.

Understanding what you are dealing with will determine who you allow to enter and exit your life. It will allow you to have clarity in who you are a problem within yourself. We all have suffered emotional trauma and that is another reason we must be truthful to those that come into our lives if we are not, we continue a vicious cycle and the revolving doors begin. The worst statements we can make is one week this is my spiritual father or mother and next month it is someone else. I would have wanted to choose others to be my spiritual parents but I would be out of order. Many I am grateful for and I honor but they did not birth me. I am tremendously thankful for every connection and the place they hold so dearly in my life, there are times they speak phenomenal life into me. I believe everything is orchestrated in the timing of God and waiting on Him is crucial, so we can walk in an area of deliverance, with no offense. Now back to the orphan spirit. This fatherless spirit. What does it look like?

Here are a few characteristics listed by Joseph Mattera. He is the author of four theological books on the kingdom of God, entitled Ruling in the Gates (2003), Kingdom Revolution (2009), Kingdom Awakening (2010) and Walk in Generational Blessings (2012). www.josephmattera.org.

- The orphan spirit operates out of insecurity and jealousy. The spirit of sonship functions out of love and acceptance. Those with an orphan spirit are constantly battling jealousy and insecurity since security originates in a secure relationship with our parents.

- The orphan spirit is jealous of his siblings. The spirit of sonship is committed to the success of his siblings.
- The orphan spirit serves God to earn the Father's love. The spirit of sonship (mature) serves God out of a sense of divine acceptance and favor.
- The orphan spirit tries to medicate his deep internal alienation through physical simulation. The mature son walks in the joy and presence of the Lord for comfort.
- The orphan spirit is driven by the need for success. The Spirit leads the mature son into his calling and mission. Many attempt to accomplish great things to satisfy the deep yearning in their hearts for their father's approval. This results in them being driven to succeed instead of being led by the Spirit, they never really become successful at anything.
- The orphan spirit has anger and fits of rage. The spirit of sonship rests in the Father's ability to control and guide the future.

Jack Frost speaks about the orphan spirit in this excerpt from his book, *Spiritual Slavery to Spiritual Sonship*, published in 2006 by Destiny Image Publishers.

"If you (or a church) have an orphan spirit, as I did for a long time, you feel as though you don't belong. Love, value, honor, and acceptance are foreign concepts to you. You believe you have to act right, dress right, talk right and do right in order to be loved and accepted; and even then, it still doesn't happen. You feel as if there is something more you have to do or put in order to find rest and feel valued. With a spirit of sonship, however, you feel loved, valued,

honored, and accepted for who you are as God's creation. You have no need to "prove" yourself to anyone. As a son or daughter, you feel a sense of total love and acceptance. Contrarily, as an orphan, you feel like you are on the outside looking in, trying as hard as you can to perform and be good enough to earn a place in someone's heart.

When wanting to cast out an orphan heart, remember that you can displace it only by introducing it to a loving Father. Even then, an orphan heart must choose to embrace the spirit of sonship by willingly becoming interdependent in relationships and embracing God's community of love. This is not a once-and-for-all choice. You choose sonship over and over because orphan thinking doesn't surrender easily, and it often comes back and tries to assert its influence once again. The orphan spirit tries constantly to weaken our families, relationships, and the nations by deceiving us into becoming subject to our own mission rather than living life to experience God's love and to give it away." There are many authors on this one topic please search for yourself but let nothing hinder you any longer to move forward."

This is a real spirit we look at and overlook or wait until it is too late. We find they are hyper-sensitive. They do not interpret reality correctly. I have found those who carry an orphan spirit interpret everything through the lenses of their abandonment, rejection, and disappointment. They can interpret reality differently than other people. Remember, leaders with an orphan spirit often use people for their own agenda rather than viewing their leadership assignment to love and empower others.

Those with an orphan spirit have a huge void in their heart that only God can fill. Until and or unless they allow the Lord to heal their woundedness, they will live life seeking the approval of others. Their pain is so great they look for temporary (superficial) relief by getting people to notice them so they can receive their accolades. Those with the orphan spirit will attack the ones that strive to assist them into their future. Simply by wanting all the attention. When parents are called to this awesome responsibility, they are called to more than one. It can't be give me more than you give this one.

A relationship will determine how each person will develop into their God-given potentials. Here are some tidbits for the spiritual parents to keep in mind when those are seeking them out to mentor, coach, or be a spiritual parent.

- Submitting to spiritual authority is difficult for them to do.
- Because of trust issues, they have trouble relying on anyone enough to receive correction, spiritual guidance or discipline. Be careful with the lone ranger spirit.
- There is turmoil within their own family. Since they have never experienced being fathered properly, they do not understand the role of a parent or how to connect emotionally to their biological parent making it hard to connect to a spiritual parent.

These matters cause extreme friction between spouses and the alienation of children. Those with an orphan spirit either view God as a relentless dominator or as a distant father who cannot be fully trusted. While growing up, they experienced abandonment from an authority figure, received harsh treatment and felt unloved. These circumstances caused them to transfer this view of their father into their relationship with God. Having a spiritual encounter with God will permeate their souls and transform their view of Father God, a true experience of the Father's love. Also, they need spiritual fathers in their lives who will represent and lead them to God giving them the opportunity to allow Him to restore their souls.

Enjoy your journey as you are prepared to be a spiritual parent and for those that are seeking a spiritual parent prepare to be parented. Breathe now and prepare to Arise and Soar!

Elder Brenda Gilbert
Destiny International Ministries

As I recollected a thought came to my mind of how my mother said I was born. She told me that the umbilical cord was wrapped around my neck and that she was in labor with me for many hours. This traumatic birth, that brought its friends of rejection and abandonment. Satan wanted me dead and my assignment aborted before I even began to live but God!

As I grew up I was always told how different I was and my mother called me her peculiar child. Today I have learned through the temperament test I am INT Personality type a Melancholic-Choleric. I am an introverted, intuitive, thinking, and judging I am shy and fearful about some things. Because of my personality and appearance, I was misunderstood a lot and was told by some I thought I was cute or something. I didn't like gossip and loud talking people. One church I attended as I grew older in my twenties called shyness a demon! And this was the knowledge of what they called deliverance with no explanation of the accusation.

Well, this watered the rejection piece in my life from school and at home. My father decided that he no longer wanted to have a family with his seven children vacated the premises. We were shocked and insulted the woman was my mother's cousin This put a hole in my angry heart and put the orphan spirit at work with the spirit of abandonment in high gear. I made inner vows when I was only a child maybe nine years old and I carried these vows into my late adulthood. I vowed to never trust men because of these vows and being hurt on numerous occasions. I built walls around my heart. There is one thing I discovered, the prison walls may have kept the people out and protected me but I could not get out as well! I was trapped with my vows of faulty thinking which God never intended for me to have.

Now I will fast forward to my deliverance. When I met Apostle Brown in 2005, I was a Christian and had been one most of my life and I was a minister of the gospel. I was overly excited that she was powerful and gentle and that she knew about deliverance and the devil. I knew I had a deliverance ministry and she could teach me to walk in what God had called me to do. God had caused our paths to cross in divine destiny, but I needed inner healing and to be delivered first. As time went on I became a part of her new ministry. She was the first person that understood me as a person and what God had called me to do. The orphan spirit made me religious, dutiful and works oriented. I loved God but I couldn't believe that he loved me nor did I trust Him. I trusted no one. This is a miserable way to live because God created us as a family and to love and fellowship with one another. Apostle Brown introduced me to the language of the orphan spirit and having an orphan heart and inner healing. I struggled for years and years. Because I never had that father image and love growing up I could not relate to God as Father I could relate to Jesus as the healer and deliver;

thus, I didn't know how to give love or receive it. Through Apostle Brown's relentless love and teaching and my desire to be free from the orphan spirit, it cannot control me! I had to hear, believe, and receive the nature of God! My difference denominational didn't emphasize knowing the character of God. They taught me that you would experience fire and hell if you sinned against God. I'd like to leave you with a quote etched in my heart from Apostle Shirley R. Brown. "I will go to Hell and back for you Brenda, you are my assignment!" I know she did in my early years at Destiny even when others wanted her to give up on me. Who does that, only the pure in heart? To be continued.

9

PRAYER

Father, we are ever so thankful for all that you have provided us through your Word, every promise is yes and amen. So today we speak restoration to those that didn't know the need of someone to speak into their lives.

We speak peace into those parenting. We pray that you show them a better way, we pray that you give them strength and balance to complete this awesome assignment. We pray that healing and deliverance are properly put in place so the sons will manifest in the earth with maturity for multiplication.

We break every generational curse in the name of Jesus that has caused frustration, intimidation. Every curse of fatherlessness, every curse of not good enough.

We build each other up in the Holy spirit for belief for the greater to fall on the son, the parent, the mentor, the coach. We pray for clarity for each so no one will mishandle one another.

We decree on today a shift in the earth and a manifestation of your children as never before.

We are thankful that you have heard our prayer, Father. Such a kind and loving Father you are to us always. We are thankful for our process We are thankful for preparation. Today we magnify and glorify you for it is a New Day.

ABOUT THE AUTHOR

∼

Shirley Robinson Brown was born and raised in West Virginia. She relocated to the state of North Carolina in 1989. She is married to Fred Edward Brown, Jr. and together they have five children and five grandchildren. Dr. Brown also has a host of spiritual sons and daughters from several states across the country. At an early age, Shirley Brown's call to ministry was nurtured. Her grandmother, the late Evangelist Ilar Gilchrist, reared her in the African Methodist Episcopal Church. Dr. Brown's Christian walk has spanned from A.M.E., Baptist, and Pentecostal Holiness, to the to the tent services of A. A. Allen, where she received her spiritual first impartation. This significant impartation led to the revelation of the mandate of healing and deliverance ministry upon her life.

Dr. Brown has a diverse ministerial background. She has preached, conducted workshops, taught seminars, and led retreats in numerous churches and conferences. Her missionary and Pastoral Care interests have led her to national locations to be of service. Dr. Brown was confirmed as a Minister of the Gospel on October 18, 1996, under the ecclesiastical order of the Full Gospel Baptist Fellowship. She received her undergraduate degree in Medical Technology and has dedicated over twenty-five years of service to that profession. Her formal theological training began with Rhema Bible School where she received a certificate in Biblical Studies. She continued to study her passion for missions and completed a Missionary Candidacy from Christians In Action in Woodland, California. Dr. Brown pursued her master's degree in Biblical Studies, and in 2006, received her Doctorate in Theology from Maskil Fellowship Bible College. Dr. Brown is a Board-Certified Christian Life Coach (BCCLC) and a Board-Certified Pastoral Counselor (BCPC) through the American Association of Christian Counselors (AACC).

She is the senior pastor of Destiny International Ministries Apostolic Training Center. She is a certified Pastor Counselor with the largest counseling accreditation in the world AACC... Dr. Brown is also the CEO of Little Destiny Literacy and Child Development Center. She is CEO of SRB Enterprises, LLC - Trucking Business.

Dr. Brown has served under the leadership of various national leaders and has ministered in foreign missions to Africa, Mexico, and South America. She is actively serving with Dale & Barbara Wentroble of International Breakthrough Ministries (IbM), and is a member of the Executive Network of IbM . She is the spiritual daughter of Bishop George Bloomer. Bishop Bloomer saw her pastoral call and sent her forth to begin the journey of pastoring. She is an EPIC TIER 1 Leader with Apostle Axel Sippach where she is actively serving; in covenant relationship with Chuck Pierce, Glory of Zion. Dr. Brown stands in fellowship with many other ministries. She works promoting unity and Kingdom-building without isms and schisms.

She now serves as a spiritual mother and covenant leader of

No-Nonsense Kingdom Alliance (NNKA) for numerous other ministries. She has been featured on the NOW Network and has appeared on the Word Network. She is also the author of "To Know Him More: Moving from Religion To Relationship". Her love for people compels her to witness to the lost, heal the brokenhearted, give hope to the hopeless, and tear down the walls of tradition. Dr. Brown's apostolic anointing breaks yokes with her message of hope, deliverance, healing, and freedom. Her favorite scripture is **Philippians 4:13** (NKJV) *"I can do all things through Christ who strengthens me."*

∼

Contact Dr. Brown
Website: www.destinyintministries.org
Email: srbrown@destinyintministries.org
Call: (919)217-8795

∼

For booking/trainings:
Contact Executive Pastor Ursula Williams
executivepastor@destinyintministries.org

www.ingramcontent.com/pod-product-compliance
Lightning Source LLC
Chambersburg PA
CBHW031215090426
42736CB00009B/924